CHINESE COOKBOOK

A Culinary Journey through Chinese Cuisine (2023 Guide for Beginners)

Molly Schuman

CONTENTS

Introduction

China has the most well-known citizens and the highest-quality, most avant-garde cuisine in the world. The common name for foods from many locations and ethnic groups in China is

Chinese food. It has a lengthy history and excellent infrastructure, rich divisions and institutions, and a distinctive theme. It represents the culmination of thousands of years of Chinese culinary history. Chinese food, usually referred to as the Chinese culinary tradition, is a key component of Chinese culture. Chinese food is one of the three major international cuisines and has a significant impact on East Asia. The ingredients come from various regions and cultural dishes.

Chinese cuisine is incredibly distinct from other cuisines from around the world. Although the ingredients and flavors of Chinese dishes can differ from place to region, the way they are prepared is essentially constant. Chinese cuisine has been around since ancient times and is well known for its distinct flavor and nutritious components. Eating Chinese food has several advantages because it utilizes less fat and uses nutrients that the body requires. In China, rice is the staple food that is included in every dish and meal. Buddhists who abstain from meat can consume vegetarian fare.

Chinese food is not only delicious but also wholesome and nourishing.

The nutrients found in Chinese cooking spices are just what a human body needs to function throughout the day. These are great sources of fiber, protein, starch, and carbs. The history of Chinese cuisine is covered in the book "Chinese Cookbook." The first chapter will provide an overview of Chinese cuisine, including its historical development from the Zhou to the Ming dynasties.

The second chapter contains recipes for breakfast and snacks to get your day off to a tasty and quick start. The third chapter contains dishes for soup, salad, and lunch to help you replenish the energy you lost while working. The fourth chapter contains supper and dessert recipes so you may prepare delectable meals for your family that also include some sweet sides and desserts.

You'll find vegetarian recipes for well-known Chinese cuisine in the last chapter. Make these dishes for your special occasions or family get-togethers. To help you justify your decision to choose Chinese food, a succinct conclusion is provided regarding picking Chinese cuisine for you and your family. Start reading "Chinese Cookbook" today to improve your culinary knowledge and abilities.

Chapter 1: Introduction to Chinese Cuisine

Chinese food evolved from many regions of China and quickly gained popularity throughout the world for its distinctive cooking method and flavor. China has eight main culinary traditions. Grain and meat make up the majority of the two key ingredients in Chinese cuisine.

For any dish, vegetables, and starch are a need. Garlic, ginger, and sesame are the essential building blocks of the majority of Chinese recipes. Every cuisine uses soy sauce to add saltiness.

1.1 History of Chinese Cuisine

China reportedly had a barbecue, fried fish, and other delicacies more than 5000 years ago, according to historical archives.

 In China during the Zhou dynasty, the main sources of food were grains including peas, buckwheat, corn, and brown rice, albeit these weren't the same as what's produced in the modern agricultural sector today. Similar to other nations, salt played an important role in daily life and cooking. Salt had already been widely utilized by then. The Zhou Dynasty had a well-known cuisine known as "Ba Zheng," which remained highly popular for generations to come. The sour flavor was eventually accepted by

the populace in the Qin period. According to historical texts, berries were another popular food at the time. Bamboo slides were discovered in temples. According to scholars, it was largely used to remove fishy or odd flavors from meat or fish. Additionally, during the Qin dynasty, cooking also included the usage of cinnamon, spring onions, canola oil, and cider.

The Han dynasty loved foods with a salty flavor. Han was a period when Chinese cuisine advanced significantly. Due to the Han Dynasty's opening of the Silk Road for traders and commercial trade, there were many "foreign-made" foods and ingredients available to people at the time, including peppers, grapefruit, oranges, hazelnuts, cardamom, pineapple, pomegranate, broccoli, lettuce, thyme, fennel, spinach, garlic, and onion. This establishes a solid foundation for the advancements in Chinese cuisine throughout the later Tang period. During the Han, Wei, northern, and Southern dynasties, Chinese cuisine developed swiftly and several well-known cuisines were created.

By the Tang era, Chinese food had already reached a certain level of excellence. To live their life at a certain time, people also had a variety of gatherings or cocktail parties.

One of the great eras in Chinese culinary history is the Song Dynasty. The menus at Bianjing and Linen included a variety of cold meals, hot dinners, soups, and ornamental dishes. The labeling of the food with North, South, Chuan, and vegetable meals suggested that institutions for different cuisines had begun to emerge.

Chinese food flourished during the Yuan, Ming, and Qing dynasties. Numerous cuisines have developed. Muslims from many ethnic groups immigrated to China during this time, and halal certification took on importance as a new type of Chinese cuisine. Manchu style and flavors were introduced to Chinese cuisine during the Qing Dynasty when a Manchu king ruled. Chilled pepper crops were introduced to China during the Ming Dynasty of this era as attractive plants. Before long, Chinese people discovered its considerable utility in cooking techniques. During that time, the spicy flavor quickly gained popularity in the provinces of Hunan and Sichuan and significantly influenced their culinary methods. There are no schools teaching Chinese food. Since the late Qing Dynasty and the arrival of foreigners in China, western culinary elements have been incorporated into Chinese cuisine. Chinese food is well-known throughout the world for its vibrant colors, delicious flavors, and superior styles.

1.2 Traditional History of Chinese Dishes

Chinese food has a history that reaches back to around 5000 BC. Over such a long time, Chinese people have developed their unique method of cooking meat. Their methods for selecting ingredients to create the best combinations, their multi-method cooking techniques, and their multidisciplinary taste management have all evolved throughout time. The ancient Chinese had a very healthy diet, and according to historical records, agriculture in China probably started around 5,000 years ago. Chinese food is characterized by changes and variations. the cuisine has always been a fundamental aspect of social interaction, and many modern dishes can be traced back to old Chinese cuisine traditions thanks to their various fragrances and flavors. The Chinese frequently equate food and art, stressing both the preparation and consumption of food.

Chinese boiling noodles are one of the key components of their entire cuisine. They can be found in many recipes in countless combinations, which has led to advancements in culinary technique over the history of the Chinese nation and national tastes. The earliest known noodles were discovered in China 4,000 years ago. Along China's Yellow River, historical relics have been discovered that contain them.

However, the East Han Dynasty, which ruled from 25 to 200 AD, is the period with the earliest conclusive historical accounts of noodles. These early noodles were often manufactured from maize flour and as time passed, their popularity increased. Noodles could be purchased from Chinese restaurants in major Chinese cities during the Song Dynasty.

As Chinese influence spread throughout Asia, noodles are widely consumed in China, Korea, the Philippines, Cambodia, Thailand, and other countries.

In Chinese culture, a big, flat-bottomed (historically stainless) spoon is used to eat sauces and other liquids while chopsticks are the primary dining utensil for real food. Wooden chopsticks are losing popularity in China and other Asian nations because of current deforestation problems; many Chinese dining establishments are considering moving to more ecologically friendly eating utensils, such as plastic or bamboo chopsticks. Silver and gold were once utilized as more opulent materials. On the other hand, plastic chopsticks made of bamboo or wood have taken the place of recycled ones in small restaurants.

One of the earliest nations in the globe to make wine is thought to be China. Since its inception, wine has served as more than just a beverage. It has been given moral and cultural significance, represented political and social life and design ideas, and even made an appearance in contemporary literature. Yellow grain wine, likely the first of its kind, was consumed by people in the Shang dynasty (16th to 12th century) to worship the gods. The production of all other varieties of wine is thought to have started during the Han and Tang periods. Years later, millet wine was introduced, and it quickly became much more popular than tea.

China consumes more pork than any other type of meat, including beef, mutton, goat, duck, and bird. The pork was consumed by Chinese citizens as early as 3000 or 4000 BC, but cattle and sheep were not native to China and were imported from West Asia shortly thereafter. Due to the high cost of beef and the vegetarian diet of Buddhist monks, many people turned to tofu, or bean paste, as a source of protein in their diets.

Bean paste, often known as tofu, has Chinese origins and is prepared from soy protein, milk, water, and a coagulant. Due to its high mineral content, low-fat content, and abundance in protein, calcium, and iron, it has been a staple meal in Chinese and Asian cuisine since the dawn of time.

Chinese doctors believed that meat was an important meal since it was a wonderful source of vitamins, but only the wealthiest could afford to eat it. A measure was created to address this, providing every resident of China with a free cup of tofu each week. Tofu is comprised of sorghum and other ingredients, including rice, and provides the same amount of protein as meat. People in ancient China might have sliced their meat into tiny pieces to prepare it because it was difficult to cook on a large scale at that time. Even in Western veggie meals, tofu has emerged as a key component.

1.3 Nutritional Information and Health Benefits of Chinese Food

Chinese cuisine is highly well-known and offers all the nutrients that the body and metabolism need to stay healthy. Chinese people do not have an obesity problem despite consuming an average of 30% more calories than Americans and following the same behavioral patterns. This is so because Chinese eating avoids foods high in sugar and low in vitamins.

In the West, veggies are "add-ons" to other meals, but in Chinese cuisine, vegetables are the main ingredient. Chinese people believe that a sizable quantity of vegetables and a modest number of animals can be adequately paired. Since meat contains more calories, it is essential. Chinese cuisine includes significantly less sugar, processed sweeteners, and high-fat ingredients, allowing our systems to detect fullness more quickly. This encourages people who eat Chinese food to eat just enough to sustain themselves rather than stuffing their bodies with too many calories. On the other hand, the Western diet deceives our bodies into staying within unhealthy borders longer than necessary.

The organism receives the energy it requires from carbohydrates to get through the day. The liver transforms them into glycogen, which is a resource that is easily accessible in the liver and muscles. Fat is an unreliable source of energy, as are other sources. Chinese cuisine also uses healthy carbs, such as rice and noodles, to keep you full without consuming too many calories.

Proteins, carbs, and other nutrients must all be included in your meal. Proteins support the maintenance and development of muscle strength, while carbs provide the necessary fuel. Chinatown cuisine is the best option because of this. In dishes, vegetables, noodles, or rice are frequently utilized, and any protein—beef, fish, or another—gives you a nutritional balance. Finding a dinner with other cultures that incorporates all these different nutritional ingredients into one dish might be challenging.

1.4 Key Ingredients to Prepare Chinese Dishes at Home

Chinese food is renowned for its abundance of well-seasoned, fried, high-fibre meals, which give the food a richer flavour.

In ancient medicine, pungent garlic was used to treat respiratory issues.

Bok choy: This member of the cabbage family is a great source of vitamins A and C, which support the immune system.

Ginger: Used for many years to stop vomiting and increase appetite, ginger has a long history of usage in traditional Chinese medicine.

Shiitake mushrooms: Shiitake mushrooms give dishes a pleasing scent and flavour. They also work perfectly as a meat alternative in some sauces, allowing you to reduce calories without sacrificing flavour.

Sesame seeds, despite their small size, are bursting with minerals including calcium, iron, and copper as well as a significant quantity of fibre.

Tofu is an excellent way to obtain a sufficient amount of protein from vegetable sources.

These items are widely used in Chinese cooking and are readily available in markets and retail establishments.

Chapter 2: Chinese Breakfast and Snack Recipes

2.1 Crispy Sesame Tofu and Broccoli

Cooking Time: 55 minutes
Serving Size: 4

Ingredients:

- ½ teaspoon salt
- ¼ teaspoon pepper
- 2 scallions
- ¾ pound broccoli florets
- 2 teaspoons sesame seeds
- 1 garlic clove
- 3 tablespoons light brown sugar
- 4 teaspoons rice vinegar
- ½ inch fresh ginger
- 1-pound extra-firm tofu
- 1/3 cup water
- 2 teaspoons corn-starch
- 1/3 cup tamari
- 1 tablespoon toasted sesame oil

- 1 tablespoon neutral oil

Method:

1. Take the tofu and rinse it with water.

2. Place broccoli in a pan, add water and cook until crisp and green.

3. Combine tamari, garlic, ginger, and spice to make tamari sauce.

4. Combine the remaining ingredients and simmer.

5. Use a spoon to add the mixture and crumble the tofu.

6. Crisp up tofu over low heat.

7. Heat the sauce just until bubbles appear.

8. Stir in the tofu and broccoli to the simmering sauce.

9. Combine for 2 minutes, then top with scallions before serving.

2.2 Chinese-Style Chicken and Mushrooms

Cooking Time: 40 minutes

Serving Size: 4

Ingredients:

- ½ teaspoon sugar
- 1 garlic clove
- 100 grams of mushrooms
- ½ cup of water
- Soy sauce
- Olive oil
- 400 grams of chicken
- 3 teaspoons corn-starch
- Salt
- Black pepper
- 2 teaspoons fresh ginger

Method:

1. In a skillet with olive oil over low heat, cook mushrooms.

2. Cut the chicken and top it with the additional ingredients.

3. Combine, then let it sit for 15 minutes.

4. In a skillet with sautéed mushrooms, saute the

chicken pieces.

5. Cook well by heating.

6. Serve alongside the sauce.

2.3 Chef John's Shrimp Toast

Cooking Time: 24 minutes

Serving Size: 4

Ingredients:

- 1 tablespoon soy sauce
- 1 egg white
- ½ teaspoon white sugar
- ½ teaspoon paprika
- ½ pound raw shrimp
- ½ cup finely sliced green onions
- 3 garlic cloves
- Salt to taste
- 4 slices white bread
- 1 teaspoon sesame seeds
- 1 tablespoon ginger root
- 1 anchovy filet
- 1 teaspoon sesame oil
- ¼ cup cilantro leaves

- 1 teaspoon Asian fish sauce
- 1 pinch cayenne pepper
- 1 cup of vegetable oil

Method:

1. In a food processor, combine all the ingredients until smooth.
2. Spread the shrimp mixture over toast that has been lightly toasted.
3. Slice the edges into thirds.
4. Fill the skillet with vegetable oil and cook the food until golden brown.
5. Add green onions and serve hot.

2.4 Chinese Chicken Wings

Cooking Time: 65 minutes
Serving Size: 12

Ingredients:

- 2 tablespoons garlic powder
- 5 pounds of chicken wings
- 2 cups soy sauce
- 2 cups brown sugar

Method:

1. Combine everything except the chicken wings.

2. Heat the mixture until all of the brown sugar has melted.

3. Add the mixture to the chicken wings, then cover the bowl with plastic wrap.

4. Refrigerate the chicken for 8 hours while it is marinated.

5. Set the oven to 365 F.

6. Bake the chicken for 45 minutes in the oven with the foil covering it.

7. Remove the foil and bake for an additional 15 minutes.

8. Present warm with sauce.

2.5 Perfect Pot Stickers

Cooking Time: 30 minutes

Serving Size: 6

Ingredients:

- ½ cup green onions
- 1 pinch cayenne pepper
- 1 ½ cups green cabbage

- 3 tablespoons fresh ginger
- 2 tablespoons soy sauce
- 1 pound pork
- 4 cloves garlic
- 1 teaspoon sesame oil

Dipping Sauce

- ¼ cup of rice vinegar
- ¼ cup of soy sauce

Dough Ingredients

- ¾ teaspoon kosher salt
- 2 ½ cups all-purpose flour
- 1 cup hot water

Frying

- 8 tablespoons water for steaming
- 6 tablespoons vegetable oil

Method:

1. Combine the pork, green onion, cabbage, pepper, garlic, ginger soy sauce, and sesame oil in a bowl. Stir with a fork.

2. Wrap in plastic and place in the fridge for an hour

to chill.

3. Prepare the dough by combining the ingredients.

4. Work dough with your hands until it is smooth and soft.

5. Wrap the dough and give it 30 minutes to rest.

6. Create sticker wrappers by cutting the dough into small pieces.

7. Add pork mixture to stickers and fold.

8. To make the dipping sauce, combine the ingredients.

9. Heat a skillet, add heated oil, and cook potstickers until golden brown.

10. Sprinkle water on the food and steam for seven minutes or until crispy.

11. Offer dipping sauce on the side.

2.6 Chinese Egg Rolls

Cooking Time: 70 minutes

Serving Size: 20

Ingredients:

- 8-ounce bamboo shoots
- 1 cup wood ear mushroom

- 4 teaspoons vegetable oil
- 3 large eggs
- 1 teaspoon sugar
- 14-ounce egg roll wrappers
- 1 egg white
- 1-pound roasted pork
- 2 green onions
- 2 ½ teaspoons soy sauce
- 4 cups oil for frying
- 1 medium head cabbage
- ½ carrot
- 1 teaspoon salt

Method:

1. Add one tablespoon of oil to the heated skillet.

2. Beat one egg and add it to the oil. Cook for 2 minutes over low heat.

3. Switch sides and cook for a further 30 seconds.

4. Put it aside, allow it to cool, and cut it into thin strips.

5. Heat the remaining ingredients in the skillet with the vegetable oil until the veggies are fully cooked.

6. Add the sliced egg to the veggies and chill for an hour.

7. Place a veggie mixture in a plastic wrapper.

8. Seal the top corners of the plastic sheet by rolling it.

9. To prevent drying, cover with plastic.

2.7 Chinese Cabbage Pork Dumplings

Cooking Time: 95 minutes

Serving Size: 10

Ingredients:

- 1 teaspoon sugar
- 1 teaspoon salt
- 2 ½ cups all-purpose flour
- 1 tablespoon scallions
- ¼ teaspoon salt
- ¾ cup of water
- ½ pound cabbage
- 1 teaspoon rice cooking wine
- 1 tablespoon ginger
- 1 pound pork sirloin

Method:

1. Combine salt and flour.

2. Add water to create a smooth, elastic dough.

3. Give it a 10-minute break.

4. Separate the dough into 50 small pieces and roll each into a thin circle.

5. Once the other ingredients have been thoroughly blended, the process slowly.

6. Combine the ingredients to form dumplings.

7. To cook, steam for 6 to 7 minutes.

2.8 Pork Dumplings

Cooking Time: 35 minutes

Serving Size: 100 dumplings

Ingredients:

- 5 cups Chinese cabbage
- 100 wonton wrappers
- 1 ¾ pounds pork
- 1 tablespoon fresh ginger root
- 3 tablespoons sesame oil
- 4 cloves garlic
- 2 tablespoons green onion
- 4 tablespoons soy sauce

- 1 egg

Method:

1. Combine the soy sauce, cabbage, green onion, ginger, garlic, egg, and sesame oil in a bow
2. Form a triangle with each wonton wrapper after adding one teaspoon of the cabbage mixture.
3. After 20 to 25 minutes of steaming, serve the dumplings hot.

2.9 Hand-Pulled Chinese Noodles

Cooking Time: 90 minutes
Serving Size: 4

Ingredients:

- 2 teaspoons chili oil
- ¼ cup of soy sauce
- black sesame seeds
- 1 Thai Chile
- 3 ½ cups all-purpose flour
- ½ teaspoon kosher salt
- 1 green onion
- 4 teaspoons toasted sesame oil

Method:

1. Combine salt and flour.

2. Make a dough by adding water.

3. After giving the dough 30 minutes to rest, cut it into little pieces.

4. Shape these fragments into skinny sticks.

5. Boil for 10 minutes, then set the rest aside.

6. Add the other ingredients to cook once the skillet is hot.

7. Include the hand-pulled noodles and simmer for a few minutes longer.

8. Provide dipping sauces.

2.10 Baked Hash Brown Cups with Eggs

Cooking Time: 27 minutes

Serving Size: 4

Ingredients:

- ½ cup shredded cheddar cheese
- chives
- ¼ teaspoon black pepper
- canola oil cooking spray
- 8 large eggs

- canola oil cooking spray
- 1 bag of hash brown potatoes
- black pepper
- 4 strips of bacon
- ½ teaspoon garlic powder
- Salt

Method:

1. Set the oven to 400 F.

2. Add seasonings to a bowl with the potatoes that have been shredded.

3. Squeeze potatoes to remove water.

4. For 20 to 25 minutes, bake potatoes in muffin tins.

5. Add beaten eggs to a heated skillet.

6. Use a rubber spatula to stir. Avoid overcooking eggs.

7. Bake the potato for 3 to 7 minutes or until the eggs and salt completely melt.

8. Dish out with sauce.

2.11 Cream Cheese Wontons

Cooking Time: 30 minutes
Serving Size: 6

Ingredients:

- 8 ounces of cream cheese
- ½ teaspoon sugar
- 24 wonton wrappers
- 1 egg beaten
- oil for frying
- 2 teaspoons minced chives
- ½ teaspoon onion powder

Method:

1. Combine and blend onion powder, cream cheese, and sugar.

2. Lay a wonton wrapper and cover it with a teaspoon of cream cheese.

3. Shape the wrapping into a package and egg-brush the edges.

4. Add four teaspoons of oil to a pan and heat it to 350 degrees.

5. Fry wonton till golden brown, about 6 to 7 minutes.

6. Place the soaked paper towel in a separate location.

7. Sauté all wonton wraps in tamari sauce and serve.

2.12 Lumpia Shanghai

Cooking Time: 25 minutes

Serving Size: 6

Ingredients:

- 3 cups cooking oil
- 50 pieces of lumpia wrapper

Filling Ingredients:

- ½ teaspoon black pepper
- ½ cup parsley
- 1 ½ lb. ground pork
- 1 tablespoon sesame oil
- 2 eggs
- 2 pieces of onion
- 1 ½ teaspoons salt
- 2 pieces of carrots
- 1 ½ teaspoon garlic powder

Method:

1. In a dish, whisk together all the filling ingredients.
2. Place fillings on a lumpia wrap.
3. Beat an egg and paint the borders with it.
4. Roll the tortillas and set them aside.

5. Drop the wrappers into the hot oil in the heated skillet.

6. Cook lumpia till it floats in the oil.

7. Dish up extra oil with sauce after soaking.

Chapter 3: Chinese Lunch, Salad, and Soup

Recipes

3.1 Seasoned Snack Mix

Cooking Time: 30 minutes
Serving Size: 10

Ingredients:

- ¼ cup Crisco Butter Flavour
- ¾ teaspoon garlic salt
- ¼ teaspoon cayenne pepper
- 2 cups oyster crackers
- 7 ounces of peanuts
- ¾ cup grated Parmesan cheese
- Salt
- ¼ teaspoon onion powder
- 3 cups of rice
- 2 teaspoons Worcestershire sauce
- 2 teaspoons Italian seasoning
- 1 square cereal
- 2 cups round toasted oat cereal

- 2 cups pretzel sticks

Method:

1. Set the oven to 325 F.

2. In the oven, melt the shortening and set it aside.

3. Combine Worcestershire sauce, seasoning, garlic, ginger, salt, and pepper in a bowl. Stir.

4. Combine the mixture with the additional ingredients and melt the shortening.

5. Combine thoroughly and distribute evenly on the baking sheet.

6. Bake for 16 to 18 minutes, stirring after 10 minutes.

7. Cool, then put things in containers.

3.2 Shao Bing - Chinese Flatbread

Cooking Time: 65 minutes
Serving Size: 4

Ingredients:

- 2 teaspoons Sichuan peppercorn
- 1 teaspoon of spices

- 1 teaspoon chicken
- ¼ teaspoon salt
- 300 grams of plain flour
- 1 tablespoon Chinese cooking wine
- ½ teaspoon salt
- 3 tablespoons vegetable oil
- ¼ cup oil
- 1 tablespoon soy sauce
- 250 grams of ground beef
- ¼ cup spring onion
- 2 teaspoons ground ginger
- ¼ cup chopped onion
- 2 teaspoons sesame oil
- ¼ cup chopped coriander
- 2 tablespoons spring onion
- 1 ½ tablespoons flour
- 2 teaspoons white pepper
- sesame seeds

Method:

1. To make the dough, combine the flour, sugar, and salt in a bowl and stir until lumpy. Add oil, water, and yeast. The dough should be worked before being wrapped in plastic. Wait 30 minutes before moving.

2. Heat oil in a small pan to make an oil paste. Add cake flour and blend well. Once aromatic, continue to cook. Observe cooling.

3. Set your oven to 425 °F.

4. When shaping bread, roll out the dough. Roll the dough once more after spreading the oil paste on it. Bread should be cut into pieces and sprinkled with sesame seeds.

5. Bake loaves for 12 to 15 minutes to get a beautiful brown crust.

6. Cut the sides and spoon sauce over them.

3.3 Crunchy Chinese Pork Salad

Cooking Time: 20 minutes

Serving Size: 4

Ingredients:

- 3 ounces chow Mein noodles
- 6 cups iceberg lettuce
- 4 slices bacon
- ½ cup green onions
- 3 tablespoons soy sauce
- 8 ounces water chestnuts

- ¾ pound roasted pork loin
- 1 tablespoon ketchup
- 2 tablespoons honey
- 1 teaspoon mustard

Method:

1. Combine and blend onion powder, cream cheese, and sugar.

2. Lay a wonton wrapper and cover it with a teaspoon of cream cheese.

3. Shape the wrapping into a package and egg-brush the edges.

4. Add four teaspoons of oil to a pan and heat it to 350 degrees.

5. Fry wonton till golden brown, about 6 to 7 minutes.

6. Place the soaked paper towel in a separate location.

7. Sauté all wonton wraps in tamari sauce and serve

3.4 Chinese Tomato and Egg Sauté

Cooking Time: 30 minutes
Serving Size: 2

Ingredients:

- 3 pinches of shredded coconut
- Black pepper
- 1 tablespoon ketchup
- 1 teaspoon of sugar
- 1 cup white rice
- ½ teaspoon sesame oil
- 1 teaspoon corn starch
- 2 scallions
- 1 heirloom tomato
- 1 tablespoon rice wine
- 2 cups of water
- 4 large eggs
- 1 pinch of salt

Method:

1. Finely chop the onion and thinly slice the tomatoes.

2. Seasonings should be added to a bowl of eggs.

3. Combine eggs and rice wine.

4. Add two tablespoons of oil to a hot wok.

5. Add the eggs and stir. Place aside

6. Add one tablespoon of oil to a hot wok.

7. Include tomatoes and chives.

8. Stir-fry with seasonings added.

9. Include cooked eggs and 1 cup of water.

10. Stir and cover for a few minutes to allow the tomatoes to paste.

11. Heat the sauce until it reaches the desired thickness.

3.5 Chinese Meat Filled Buns (Baozi)

Cooking Time: 1 hour 45 minutes
Serving Size: 16

Ingredients:

- 3 tablespoons sugar
- 1 teaspoon salt
- 50 milliliters cold water

- 300 grams pork (or chicken)
- 1 teaspoon fresh ginger
- 3 cloves garlic
- 2 spring onion
- 1 tablespoon rice wine
- 1 teaspoon sugar
- 3 shiitake mushrooms
- 2 tablespoons soy sauce
- 1 tablespoon oyster sauce
- 400 grams flour
- 1 ½ teaspoons baking powder
- ½ teaspoon sesame oil
- 3 tablespoons pork lard
- 190 milliliters warm water
- 2 teaspoons yeast

Method:

1. Combine the flour, yeast, sugar, salt, and baking powder.

To make the dough, combine warm water and melted fat.

3. Let it rest for 30 minutes, then smooth it out.

4. Combine the remaining ingredients in a blender.

5. Separate the dough into small pieces.

6. Cut the pieces into circles, then add the filling.

7. Form a bun again, then lay it away for 30 minutes.

8. Steam buns on greaseproof paper to prevent them from sticking to the steamer's sides.

9. Steam for 15 to 20 minutes or until the product is glossy and has a bun-like texture.

10. Serve alongside lettuce and sauce.

3.6 Snack Dippers with Hillshire Farm Smoked Sausage

Cooking Time: 35 minutes
Serving Size: 10

Ingredients:

- 2 tablespoons yellow mustard
- 1 tablespoon honey
- ¼ cup packed brown sugar
- ¼ cup mayonnaise
- ¼ teaspoon black pepper
- 14 ounces Smoked Sausage

Method:

1. Unwrap the sausages and place them on a tray. For 30 minutes, freeze.

2. Slice sausages into pieces measuring 1/4 inch on a cutting board.

3. Preheat the oven to 325 F.

4. Add brown sugar to the baking dish and add the sausages.

5. Sausages should be lightly browned after 20 minutes in the oven.

6. Combine all other ingredients in a bowl, then serve sausages dipped.

3.7 Chinese Pork Salad

Cooking Time: 10 minutes

Serving Size: 6

Ingredients:

- ½ cup stir-fry sauce
- ½ red onion
- 3 ounces chow Mein noodles

- 20 ounces pea pods
- 8 ounces mandarin oranges
- 1 pound pork strips (stir-fry)

Method:

1. For 25 minutes, marinate pork strips in the marinade.

2. In a big skillet, stir-fry the pork for 6 to 7 minutes.

3. In a bowl, combine the remaining ingredients.

4. Combine the mixture with pork sauce.

5. Mix and plate.

3.8 Yang Chow Fried Rice

Cooking Time: 25 minutes
Serving Size: 6

Ingredients:

- 2 large eggs
- 4 cups day-old rice
- 1 teaspoon toasted sesame oil
- ½ teaspoon kosher salt
- ½ teaspoon chicken bouillon

- ½ pound Chinese BBQ pork
- 3 scallions
- ½ teaspoon white pepper
- 3 tablespoons vegetable oil
- ¼ pound shrimp
- 1 tablespoon soy sauce
- 2 tablespoons oyster sauce

Method:

1. In 1 tablespoon of frying oil, fried shrimp. Place aside.

2. Soften scallions and chicken bouillon in a saucepan.

3. Make a hole in the centre of the rice and add it to a wok.

4. Add the beaten egg and thoroughly combine the rice.

5. Stir-fry the chicken mixture with the additional ingredients to create a paste.

6. Spread the paste over the rice. Serve warm.

3.9 Chinese-Style Spareribs

Cooking Time: 2 hours

Serving Size: 6

Ingredients:

- 3 tablespoons dry sherry
- 2 cloves garlic
- 6 pounds pork spareribs
- 2 tablespoons honey
- 2 tablespoons soy sauce
- ¼ cup hoisin sauce
- ¼ cup of water

Method:

1. Split the spareribs into pieces.

2. In a bowl, combine each item.

3. Place ribs inside a sizable sealing bag.

4. Remove 1/4 cup of the mixture and set it aside.

5. Fill the bag with the ribs and add the remaining ingredients.

6. Marinate the mixture for an hour in the fridge.

7. Grab a baking pan and preheat the oven to 350°F.

8. Arrange the ribs on a baking sheet and bake for 90 minutes.

9. Take off the sheet and use a brush to apply the remaining 1/4 cup of the mixture on the ribs.

10. Add 30 more minutes to the bake.

11. Hot with sauce to serve.

3.10 Soya Sauce Mushroom Chicken with Braised Eggs

Cooking Time: 105 minutes

Serving Size: 1

Ingredients:

- 4 cloves garlic
- 1 teaspoon sesame oil
- 4 eggs
- 3 pieces of chicken thighs
- 150 milliliters chicken broth
- 3 pieces of rock sugar
- 1 tablespoon cornflour
- 3 slices ginger
- 1 tablespoon Chinese cooking wine

- potato
- 6 button mushrooms
- 2-star anise
- 3 tablespoons light soy sauce
- 2 tablespoons dark soy sauce
- 1 dash pepper
- 1 cinnamon stick

Method:

Wash the chicken, then pat it dry with a cloth.

2. Clean the mushrooms and give the chicken a 30-minute marinade.

3. An hour of mushroom soaking.

4. Add ginger, garlic, anise, and cinnamon sticks to hot oil.

5. Stir-fry the chicken for 5 minutes.

6. Include the mushrooms and cook the chicken with them for 10 minutes.

7. Stir in all the other vegetables.

8. After more than 20 minutes of simmering, add additional ingredients.

9. To thicken the sauce, add cornflour and serve it hot.

3.11 Loaded Breakfast Baked Potatoes

Cooking Time: 80 minutes
Serving Size: 4

Ingredients:

- 4 russet potatoes
- teaspoons salt
- teaspoons black pepper
- 2 scallions
- 1 tablespoon butter
- 4 large eggs
- 4 strips bacon
- 2 ounces cheddar cheese
- ½ teaspoon salt
- ¼ teaspoon black pepper
- Sour cream
- Hot sauce

Method:

1. Preheat an aluminium foil in the oven to 400°F.

2. Place potatoes on a sheet of aluminium foil after forking them.

3. Bake potatoes in the oven for 60 to 70 minutes.

4. To add fillings, take the potato and cut it lengthwise.

5. Add the remaining ingredients and heat the skillet.

6. Continue stirring while cooking.

7. Fill potatoes with the mixture and bake for 10 minutes.

8. Serve right away.

3.12 Steamed Halibut Fillet with Ginger and Scallions

Cooking Time: 45 minutes
Serving Size: 4

Ingredients:

- 3 scallions
- 2 tablespoons canola oil
- 4 tablespoons water
- 2 inches fresh ginger
- 1 tablespoon chicken powder
- 2 ½ pounds fillets
- ¼ teaspoon salt
- 2 teaspoons sugar

- 4 baby bok choy
- vegetable oil cooking spray
- 3 tablespoons lite soy sauce
- 4 Chinese black mushrooms
- ¼ teaspoon black pepper

Method:

1. Process all ingredients in a food processor until just barely smooth.

2. Blend again after adding eggs.

3. Put a lemon slice on each of the steamed fish fillets.

4. After boiling water, let it steam for three to four minutes. Avoid overcooking.

5. Spread the sauce over the fillets on a plate. At room temperature, cool. Add spinach leaves to the dish.

3.13 Chicken Mustard Green Congee

Cooking Time: 55 minutes
Serving Size: 6

Ingredients:

- ¼ cup mustard greens
- 1 tablespoon sesame oil

- 2 garlic cloves
- ¼ cup chives
- 12 ounces chicken tenderloin
- 1 ginger
- ¾ cup sweet rice
- ½ teaspoon dark soy sauce

Method:

1. Simmer the chicken with ginger and garlic in a pot.

2. Cook the chicken for 20 minutes to ensure adequate cooking.

3. Remove ginger and garlic and shred the chicken.

4. Add the rice to the boiling chicken broth and simmer for 25 minutes.

5. Add other ingredients and simmer for an additional five minutes.

6. After 10 minutes of resting, serve.

3.14 Energy Snack Cake

Cooking Time: 85 minutes

Serving Size: 4

Ingredients:

- 300 grams walnut pieces
- 100 grams flour
- 60 grams of dried cranberries
- 10 dried figs
- ½ teaspoon baking soda
- ¼ teaspoon baking powder
- 3 large eggs
- 15 grams of dried dates
- 80 grams of dried apricots
- ½ teaspoon salt
- 140 grams of sugar
- 1 teaspoon vanilla extract

Method:

1. Combine flour, salt, baking soda, and baking powder in a bowl.

2. Add sugar, almonds, and dried fruit to the mixture.

3. Bring the oven to 150 °F.

4. Whisk together the eggs and vanilla essence in a small bowl.

5. Stir well before adding the egg mixture to the flour mixture.

6. Combine additional components and pour them into a baking dish.

7. Bake for sixty to seventy minutes.

8. After it has cooled, slice it.

3.15 Taco Snack Mix

Cooking Time: 16 minutes

Serving Size: 4

Ingredients:

- 2 cups crackers
- 2 cups of corn chips
- 2 cups Rice Chex Cereal
- 1 package McCormick Taco
- Seasoning Mix
- 2 cups Wheat Chex Cereal
- ½ cup unsalted butter

Method:

1. Melt butter in the microwave for 40 seconds.

2. Combine cereal, corn chips, and cheese crackers in a bowl.

3. Stir well after adding the seasoning to the mixture.

4. Cook the mixture in the microwave, uncovered, for 6 to 8 minutes.

5. Let cool at ambient temperature.

3.16 One-Bowl Caramel Snack Cake with Caramel Glaze

Cooking Time: 60 minutes

Serving Size: 9

Ingredients:

- ¾ cup cake flour
- 1 ½ teaspoons baking powder
- ¼ cup confectioners' sugar
- 1 large egg
- 2 large egg yolks
- cooking oil spray

- ¾ cup unsalted butter
- ¾ teaspoon salt

For Cake

- 1 cup dark brown sugar
- 1 cup heavy cream
- 1 tablespoon vanilla extract
- 1 cup all-purpose flour

For Caramel

- ½ cup heavy cream
- 1 teaspoon flaky sea salt
- 1 teaspoon vanilla extract
- 1 cup dark brown sugar

Method:

1. Preheat the oven to 350 degrees Fahrenheit and grease the pan. Place aside.

2. Microwave 14 cups of butter until it melts.

3. Mix the remaining butter with the brown sugar.

4. Heat for 1 minute while stirring. Until the caramel thickens, microwave for more than a minute. Set aside so you can relax.

5. Combine the ingredients in powder form with the caramel.

6. Use a rubber spatula to mix everything.

7. Bake on the center rack for 20 minutes.

8. After rotating the baking dish, bake the food for over 20 minutes or until it softens.

9. Spread the cake with the remaining butter and caramel.

10. After 10 minutes of cooling, cut it into pieces.

3.17 Wheat Bread Snack

Cooking Time: 10 minutes
Serving Size: 4

Ingredients:

- watercress
- 1 slice whole-wheat bread
- olive oil
- 1 cup skimmed milk

Method:

1. Toast the bread until it is golden brown.

2. Spread toast with olive oil and watercress.

3. Milk is recommended.

3.18 Hot and Sour Soup

Cooking Time: 1 hour 15 minutes
Serving Size: 4

Ingredients:

- 1 ½ tablespoon vinegar
- Salt
- 60 grams prawns
- 1 tablespoon soya sauce
- ½ tablespoon chili powder
- 5 grams of carrot
- 5 grams of cabbage
- 1 Egg
- 1 tablespoon coriander
- 1 teaspoon chili oil
- 5 grams of bamboo shoots
- 5 grams black mushrooms
- 5 grams button mushrooms
- 100 grams of chicken
- ½ teaspoon white pepper

- 2 tablespoon cornflour
- 5 grams of bean sprouts
- 5 grams of fresh beans
- 2 cups stock

Method:

1. Tear up all the produce, the prawns, and the fowl.

2. In a pan, cook the chicken and all the vegetables.

3. Fill the wok with the remaining ingredients and seasonings.

4. Finish the thick soup by stirring in the cornflour and egg.

3.19 Cantonese Chicken Soup

Cooking Time: 40 minutes

Serving Size: 2

Ingredients:

- 5 spoons large chicken stock
- 10 Mushrooms
- 1 whole chicken
- 5 Pieces bok choy

- 3-4 spring onions

Method:

1. Remove the chicken's skin, then cut the meat into 10 to 12 large slices.

2. Split each mushroom in half.

3. Arrange the chicken, mushrooms, and bok choy in a uniform layer in a container.

4. Include chicken stock and simmer for a full hour.

5. As needed, add the remaining ingredients and water.

6. Continue to cook after 20 minutes.

7. Add cornflour to the soup to thicken it.

3.20 Vegetable Manchow Soup

Cooking Time: 35 minutes
Serving Size: 2

Ingredients:

- 2 tablespoon French beans
- 2 tablespoon Carrots

- 2 Spring onions
- 1 teaspoon Pepper
- 4 Cups Water
- 2 tablespoon Mushrooms
- 1 teaspoon Ginger
- 1 teaspoon Garlic
- 1 teaspoon green chilies
- 2 stems Spring onion
- Oil and salt
- 1 tablespoon Coriander leaves
- 2 tablespoon Cabbage
- 1 tablespoon Soya sauce
- 4 tablespoon Cornflour
- 1 cup Water
- 2 tablespoon Capsicum

Method:

1. For two minutes, stir-fry ginger, green chilies, garlic, and coriander leaves.

All vegetables should be cut up and added to the ginger-garlic combination.

3. Include sauces and seasonings. Cook for longer than five minutes.

4. After adding the water, wait until it begins to boil.

5. Combine hot water and cornflour in a small bowl.

6. Stir the cornflour mixture into the vegetable and boiling water mixture.

7. Stir until the sauce begins to thicken.

8. Discard the heat and top with green onions.

Chapter 4: Chinese Dinner and Desserts Recipes

4.1 Chinese BBQ Pork

Cooking Time: 20 minutes

Serving Size: 4

Ingredients:

- 1 tablespoon honey
- 2 teaspoons fresh ginger root
- ½ cup dry sherry
- 8 drops red food colouring
- 2 pounds pork loin roast
- 1 teaspoon sesame oil
- 1 whole scallion
- 3 tablespoons soy sauce
- 2 ½ tablespoons hoisin sauce

Method:

1. Slice the pork thinly.

2. Grease a basin for cooking with oil.

3. Combine all the ingredients in the cooker.

4. Cook on low heat for 7 hours with a cover on.

5. Put fried rice on the table.

4.2 Yam Bean, Carrot, and Cucumber Snack

Cooking Time: 45 minutes

Serving Size: 3

Ingredients:

- Worcestershire sauce
- Peanuts
- 2 carrots
- ½ yam bean
- Unflavoured gelatine
- Hot sauce
- Lime juice
- Japanese peanuts
- 1 cucumber
- 6 limes

Method:

1. Grate the carrot, cucumber, and yam beans. Drain everything.

2. Spread beans in an oiled baking pan.

3. Disperse lime and gelatin. Firmly press.

4. Continue with step 4 to add a layer of cucumber and carrots.

5. Put the lid on and freeze for 30 minutes.

6. Combine additional ingredients to create a sauce.

7. Add a topping of peanuts.

4.3 Stir-Fried Tofu with Rice

Cooking Time: 30 minutes

Serving Size: 6

Ingredients:

- 8 ounces of cream cheese
- ½ teaspoon sugar
- 24 wonton wrappers
- 1 egg beaten
- oil for frying
- 2 teaspoons minced chives
- ½ teaspoon onion powder

Method:

1. Combine and blend onion powder, cream cheese, and sugar.

2. Lay a wonton wrapper and cover it with a teaspoon

of cream cheese.

3. Shape the wrapping into a package and egg-brush the edges.

4. Add four teaspoons of oil to a pan and heat it to 350 degrees.

5. Fry wonton till golden brown, about 6 to 7 minutes.

6. Place the soaked paper towel in a separate location.

7. Sauté all wonton wraps in tamari sauce and serve

4.3 Stir-Fried Tofu with Rice

Cooking Time: 40 minutes

Serving Size: 2

Ingredients:

For the Tofu

- 100 grams of tofu
- 1-inch ginger
- 3 Garlic cloves
- 1-inch red onion
- 1 Lemongrass stick
- 2 Shallots
- A handful of coriander leaves
- 1 teaspoon refined oil

- 2 teaspoon soya sauce
- 2 teaspoon chilli paste
- 2 teaspoon honey

For the Fried Rice

- 2 teaspoon soya sauce
- ½ Lemon
- Carrots
- Coriander leaves
- 1 teaspoon olive oil
- Spring onions
- Salt and pepper
- 1 fresh red chilly
- 1 Ginger

Method:

1. Stir well after adding the chopped mariner to the heating pan.

2. Include ginger, shallots, garlic, and spices.

3. Include chilli paste, honey, and soy sauce.

4. Use a rubber spatula to combine the coriander. Place aside.

5. In a pan, combine carrot, onion, salt, pepper, and ginger.

6. After drizzling in the oil, add the chile, lemon juice, and soy sauce.

7. Cook the rice for seven more minutes after adding the coriander.

8. Present rice.

4.4 Dim Sums

Cooking Time: 1 hour 20 minutes
Serving Size: 4

Ingredients:

For Chicken and Prawn Dumplings

- 5 ml sesame oil
- 2.5 grams white pepper
- 150 grams of chicken
- Wonton skin
- Potato starch
- 150 grams prawn
- 5 grams of sugar

- Salt

For Vegetable Coriander Dumplings

- 10 grams of water chestnuts
- 10 grams of carrots
- 10 grams button mushrooms
- 5 grams of sugar
- 10 grams garlic
- 10 grams of bamboo shoots
- 5 grams sesame oil
- 10 ml of oil
- 10 grams brown garlic

For Wonton Skin

- Salt
- 50 grams of wheat starch
- Potato starch

Method:

1. Combine the salt, potato starch, sesame oil, and sugar with the chicken and prawns.

2. Fill the wonton skin with the mixture and steam it. With soy sauce, please.

3. Combine all ingredients for the dumplings except the wonton skin.

4. Fill wonton skin with the mixture and steam. Accompanied by the sauce.

5. Combine potato with wheat starch, salt, and water to make wonton skin.

6. Stir in potato starch until it becomes thicker.

7. Divide into pieces, then roll into balls. Insert fillings.

8. Fry the garlic in oil for the sauce. Make a paste out of soaked chillies.

9. When the garlic becomes brown, add the chilli paste. Include seasonings.

4.5 Quick Noodles

Cooking Time: 45 minutes
Serving Size: 2

Ingredients:

- 1 cup carrot, julienne
- 1 tablespoon vegetable oil
- 1 cup onion
- 1 cup spring onions

- 2 packets noodles
- 1 tablespoon ginger and garlic chili
- paste
- 1 tablespoon coriander
- 1 tablespoon lemon juice
- 1 teaspoon vinegar
- 1 tablespoon soy sauce
- 1 tablespoon schezwan sauce
- 1 cup pepper
- 1 cup mushrooms
- ½ lettuce
- ½ teaspoon turmeric powder
- 1 teaspoon sugar

Method:

1. Prepare noodles as directed on the package. Drain the water, then chill in it.

2. Add oil to the mixture and stir to prevent the noodles from clinging to one another.

3. Get a wok's oil hot.

4. Combine vegetables, soy sauce, mushroom, ginger, and garlic paste in a wok.

5. Stir the remaining ingredients together in a small dish.

6. Add noodles and this mixture to the veggie mixture. Mix well.

7. Add chopped coriander as a garnish and serve.

4.6 Szechuan Chili Chicken

Cooking Time: 45 minutes

Serving Size: 8

Ingredients:

- 3 tablespoon brown peppercorn
- Salt
- 2-3 spring onions
- 2 teaspoon white pepper
- 5-6 dry red chilies
- 2-3 tablespoon ginger
- 3 tablespoon green peppercorn
- 10-12 pieces chicken
- 1 tablespoon black vinegar
- 2 teaspoon chili oil
- Oil for frying

Method:

1. Brown the chicken after frying it with ginger.

2. Drain the oil and reserve it.

3. Include brown peppercorn, onion, garlic, and peppercorns.

4. After 5 minutes of sautéing, add spices.

5. Add black vinegar after stirring for more than 10 minutes.

6. Fry for over ten minutes and add peppercorns as a garnish.

4.7 Shitake Fried Rice with Water Chestnuts

Cooking Time: 25 minutes

Serving Size: 2

Ingredients:

- 1 cup Shitake mushroom
- 1 tablespoon Ginger
- A pinch of White pepper
- 1 big drop of Sesame oil
- 1 cup rice (cooked)

- Green chilies
- 2-3 tablespoon Vegetable oil
- 4 cloves garlic
- 2-3 Water chestnuts
- 1 big tablespoon Celery
- ½ Medium Onion
- 1 big tablespoon Leeks
- Small bunch Parsley
- A dash of Rice wine vinegar
- 1 big drop of Sesame oil
- Salt to season
- 1 stalk of Spring onions

Method:

1. Prepare a stir-fry and add it to the bowl.

2. Add one tablespoon of vegetable oil to a hot pan.

3. Include leeks, onion, and celery in the oil.

4. Include ginger, chestnuts, and mushrooms.

5. Include the rice, onion, sauces, and any ingredients.

6. Stir cook, then add to bowl.

4.8 Chicken with Chestnuts

Cooking Time: 45 minutes
Serving Size: 4

Ingredients:

- 5 dried Chinese mushrooms
- 1 tablespoon fish sauce
- 1 tablespoon date puree
- 1 diced green capsicum
- 2 tablespoon sesame oil
- ½ kg chicken mince
- 1 diced red capsicum
- 3 tablespoon white radish
- 50 ml of water
- ½ teaspoon chili flakes
- 12-14 peeled water chestnuts
- 2 tablespoon chopped spring onion
- 1 tablespoon chopped garlic
- 1 tablespoon vinegar
- 1 iceberg lettuce
- 1 tablespoon shredded ginger
- 1 tablespoon soya sauce
- 1 tablespoon chopped coriander

Method:

1. Remove mushroom stems and soak mushrooms for 30 minutes in boiling water.

2. In a wok with heated oil, cook chicken with ginger until just browned.

3. Sauté the ginger, garlic, and pepper for three minutes.

4. Heat the pan and add the chicken.

5. Combine the chicken with the remaining ingredients, excluding the lettuce and coriander.

6. Stir in the veggies.

7. Add lettuce and coriander leaves as garnish.

4.9 Honey Chili Potato

Cooking Time: 35 minutes

Serving Size: 2

Ingredients:

For Frying Potatoes

- 5 tablespoon Cornflour
- 2 Potatoes
- 1 ½ tablespoon Salt

- 2 teaspoon Chili Powder

For Honey Chili Sauce

- 4 teaspoon Sesame Seeds
- 2 tablespoon Honey
- 1 teaspoon Chili Flakes
- 2 Bulbs Spring Onions
- 1 ½ teaspoon Garlic
- 1 teaspoon Vinegar
- 2 teaspoon Tomato Sauce
- 2 teaspoon Chili Sauce
- 1 teaspoon Ginger
- 2 Whole Red Chilies
- 1 teaspoon salt

Method:

1. Separate two potatoes into slices along the length.

2. Wash them thoroughly and immerse them for 15 minutes.

3. Place the slices in a basin with the salt, corn-starch, pepper, and coriander leaves.

4. Blend thoroughly until sticky.

5. Heat three tablespoons of oil in a frying pan.

6. Fry potatoes in oil till crispy and golden brown.

7. Avoid frying on high heat because it can result in

potatoes that are burned on the outside and undercooked on the inside.

8. After thoroughly cooking, set aside.

9. Heat sesame seeds in a separate frying pan until golden brown. Place aside.

10. Add tomato sauce, ginger, garlic, chilli flakes, and red chillies to a pan of heated oil.

11. Add salt, vinegar, honey, and chilli sauce after thoroughly stirring.

12. Make the sauce by stirring.

13. Stir in the fried potatoes with the sauce.

14. Spoon juice over potatoes.

4.10 Peri-Peri Chicken Satay

Cooking Time: 25 minutes

Serving Size: 2

Ingredients:

- 50 grams Peri-Peri sauce
- 100 grams of potato fries
- 100 grams of yogurt
- 200 grams of chicken thigh
- salt and pepper
- 5 grams of chili powder

- Oil to fry
- 25 grams ginger garlic paste
- 5 grams coriander leaves

Method:

1.Skewers should be soaked for one hour.

2. Combine the following in a bowl: ginger, garlic, salt, pepper, Peri-Peri sauce, chile, and garlic.

3. Stir well, then add the chicken.

4. Marinate in a sealed bag for two hours.

5. Turn the grill's heat to medium.

6. Grill the chicken and spray it with oil to avoid sticking.

7. Brown the meat on the grill for 15 to 20 minutes.

8. Include crispy potato fries with the chicken.

4.11 Garlic Soya Chicken

Cooking Time: 35 minutes

Serving Size: 2

Ingredients:

- ¼ teaspoon White Pepper
- 1 teaspoon Ginger Juice
- 450 Gram Chicken Breast
- 1 teaspoon Sesame Oil
- 1 tablespoon ginger, grated
- 1 tablespoon Rice Vinegar
- 2 tablespoon Vegetable oil
- A handful of Snow Peas
- 2 tablespoon Soy Sauce
- 5-6 Garlic cloves
- ½ Cup Red Onion
- 1 teaspoon Red Chili Flakes
- ½ Red Bell Pepper

For the Sauce

- 2 teaspoon Chinese Rice Wine
- ½ tablespoon Brown Sugar
- 1 teaspoon Cornflour
- 2 teaspoon Dark Soy Sauce

Method:

1. Slice the chicken thinly.

2. Combine the chicken in a big bowl with the white pepper and sesame oil.

3. For 15 to 20 minutes, marinate the chicken.

4. Combine all sauce ingredients in a small basin. Stir well.

5. Heat a frying pan gently. Spread 2 tablespoons of oil in a frying pan.

6. After waiting for 5 minutes, gradually add the chicken pieces to the frying pan.

7. Keep the flame at a low level. Hold off until the chicken's sides have a light brown color.

8. Stir the chicken until it browns on all sides, then remove it from the frying pan right away.

9. Increase the heat, add the red onion, and cook the peas for one minute.

10. Stir regularly to avoid overheating or burning.

11. Add bell pepper and cook for an additional 30 seconds.

12. Combine all ingredients thoroughly, then add chicken when the vegetables start to become crispy.

13. Prepare the sauce components and simmer them for a smooth, gooey consistency.

14. Cover the chicken and veggies with sauce.

15. Stir in a tablespoon of water and boil for two minutes, or until thick and bubbling.

16. Served with lettuce and fried rice.

4.12 Shrimp Fried Rice

Cooking Time: 20 minutes
Serving Size: 6

Ingredients:

- 1 package frozen mixed vegetables
- 1-pound medium shrimp
- 4 tablespoons butter
- 4 large eggs
- ¼ teaspoon pepper
- 8 bacon strips
- 3 cups cold cooked rice
- ½ teaspoon salt

Method:

1. Place a big skillet on a low heat.

2. Include 1 tablespoon of butter or vegetable oil.

Pour the beaten eggs into the skillet.

4. Stir to ensure even cooking. Take out of skillet and place aside.

5. Add vinegar to the melted butter in the skillet.

6. Place the cooked shrimp and rice in the skillet.

7. Stir and boil the shrimp for 5 minutes, or until the color turns pink.

8. Break up the eggs and put them to the skillet. Using a low flame, cook.

9. After 5 minutes, turn off the heat and top with coriander leaves.

4.13 Ginger-Cashew Chicken Salad

Cooking Time: 30 minutes
Serving Size: 8

Ingredients:

- ¼ teaspoon cayenne pepper
- 4 chicken breast halves
- ½ cup cider vinegar
- 2 teaspoons soy sauce
- 1 teaspoon salt
- ½ cup molasses
- ½ cup canola oil
- 2 tablespoons minced fresh
- gingerroot

For Salad

- 2 tablespoons sesame seeds
- 1 can mandarin oranges
- 1 cup shredded red cabbage
- 3 green onions
- 2 cups Chow Mein noodles
- 8 ounces fresh baby spinach
- ¾ cup salted cashews
- 2 medium carrots

Method:

1. Process all the ingredients, excluding the chicken, in a blender.

2. Place the processed ingredients over the chicken in a bowl.

3. Combine and marinate the chicken for three hours.

4. After preheating the broiler, add the chicken.

5 minutes of boiling. 15 additional minutes of boiling after switching sides.

6. Make noodles and slice the salad's contents.

7. Include the chicken, salad, and noodles in a different dish. Serve alongside sauce.

4.14 Beef and Spinach Lo Mein

Cooking Time: 30 minutes

Serving Size: 5

Ingredients:

- 1 tablespoon water
- 4 teaspoons canola oil
- 1 can sliced water chestnuts
- ¼ cup hoisin sauce
- 2 tablespoons soy sauce
- 1 pound beef top round steak
- 1 package fresh spinach
- 1 red chili pepper
- 6 ounces Spaghetti
- 2 teaspoons sesame oil
- 2 garlic cloves
- ¼ teaspoon crushed red pepper
- flakes
- 2 green onions

Method:

1. Combine water, sesame oil, garlic, hoisin, and soy sauce.

2. Divide 1/4 cup of the mixture into a big basin.

3. Stir in the beef before serving. 10 minutes of room temperature marinating.

4. Prepare pasta as directed on the packet.

5. Lightly heat a skillet. Include canola oil.

6. Gradually stir in the beef mixture. Don't pour the entire mixture into the skillet.

7. Stir-fry the meat mixture till it turns pink. Repeat with the remaining mixture after removing.

8. Add the remaining ingredients and hoisin mixture to a hot skillet.

9. 15 minutes of cooking. Add the beef mixture.

10. Stir in the spaghetti. Serve hot after 5 minutes of cooking.

4.15 Ginger Pork Lettuce Wraps

Cooking Time: 30 minutes
Serving Size: 2 dozen

Ingredients:

- 1 tablespoon sesame oil
- 24 Boston lettuce leaves
- 1-pound lean ground pork

- 1 can sliced water chestnuts
- 4 green onions
- 1 medium onion
- ¼ cup hoisin sauce
- 1 tablespoon red wine vinegar
- 1 tablespoon reduced-sodium soy
- sauce
- 2 teaspoons Thai chili sauce
- 4 garlic cloves
- 1 tablespoon fresh ginger root

Method:

1. Cook pork and onion in a big skillet for 10 minutes.

2. When the pink hue has disappeared and the onions are soft, remove.

3. Divide into crumbles after cutting.

4. Combine the hoisin sauce, soy sauce, vinegar, garlic, and ginger.

5. After adding the last few ingredients, cook for 10 minutes.

6. Arrange the mixture and the meat on the lettuce leaves. Fold and dish.

4.16 Asparagus Beef Sauté

Cooking Time: 30 minutes

Serving Size:

Ingredients:

- 1-pound fresh asparagus
- 1 tablespoon canola oil
- 2 garlic cloves
- 1 green onion
- ½ teaspoon salt
- 1 ½ teaspoon lemon juice
- Hot cooked rice
- ½ pound sliced fresh mushrooms
- 1 pound beef tenderloin (¾ -inch
- cubes)
- ¼ teaspoon pepper
- ¼ cup butter
- 1 tablespoon reduced-sodium soy
- sauce

Method:

1. Season the beef with salt and pepper.

2. Pour one tablespoon of cooking oil into a frying pan.

3. Include ginger and garlic. 2 minutes of stirring.

4. Include the beef and cook for 10 minutes, until just lightly browned.

5. Take out of the pan and place aside. Stay warm.

6. Place mushrooms in the same skillet with 1 tablespoon oil.

When the asparagus is tender, add it in step 7. Cook for 10 more minutes after adding the last few ingredients.

8. Include meat. After two minutes of heating, remove. Serve with rice after being set aside.

4.17 Chinese Almond Cookies

Cooking Time: 40 minutes

Serving Size: 30

Ingredients:

- ½ teaspoon baking soda
- 2 cups flour
- ½ teaspoon baking powder
- ¼ teaspoon salt
- 2 ½ teaspoons almond extract
- 30 whole almonds

- ½ cup shortening
- ¾ cup white sugar
- 1 egg
- ½ cup butter
- 1 egg beaten

Method:

1. Preheat the oven to 325°F.

2. Add flour to a sizable bowl.

3. Stir in salt thoroughly.

4. Include baking powder and soda. Stir thoroughly.

5. Combine butter, shortening, and sugar in a small bowl.

6. Blend the butter mixture after adding the almond and egg.

7. Blend the flour mixture until smooth and add.

8. Knead the dough and divide it in half.

9. Let food chill for two hours.

10. Split the dough lengthwise into 14 to 15 pieces.

11. Spray the cookie tray with cooking spray and roll each piece into a sphere.

12. Place almonds in the center of each ball after placing them in a cookie tray.

13. Use a brush to apply beaten egg to cookies.

14. Bake until golden brown for 15 to 20 minutes.

15. Take out and allow it to cool. When crisp and chilled, serve.

4.18 Nian Gao

Cooking Time: 60 minutes
Serving Size: 10

Ingredients:

- 2 ½ cups milk
- One can of red azuki beans
- 16 ounces mochiko sweet rice flour
- 1 to 1 ¾ cup sugar
- 1 tablespoon baking soda
- ½ cup unsalted butter
- ¾ cup of vegetable oil
- 3 eggs

Method:

1. Preheat the oven to 350°F.

2. Apply butter or oil to a pan using a brush or spray.

3. In a food processor, combine all the ingredients but the beans and process until smooth.

4. Place half the batter in the baking dish and sprinkle with mochiko flour.

5. Cover beans on top with another layer of batter.

6. Bake until done, about 40 to 45 minutes.

7. Use a toothpick to test the doneness of the baking.

8. Offer chilled.

4.19 Eight Treasure Rice Pudding

Cooking Time: 105 minutes

Serving Size: 8

Ingredients:

For the Rice

- 1 cup black raisins
- 1 cup yellow raisins
- ¼ teaspoon salt

For the Fruit

- Neutral oil for coating bowl
- 2 cups glutinous rice
- 1 tablespoon sunflower oil

- 1 cup sugar-glazed cherries
- 1 dried apricot

For the Filling

- 1 cup sugar lotus seeds
- 100 grams red bean paste

For the Starch Water

- 3 tablespoons water
- 2 teaspoon potato starch
- For the Sugar Syrup
- 1 tablespoon honey
- 1 tablespoon sugar
- ½ cup of water

Method:

1. Fill a sizable bowl with rice.

2. Include cold water, cover, and wait an hour.

3. Rice should be drained, soaked, and steamed for 40 minutes over simmering water.

4. Include salt and oil. Rice should not break during the mixing process.

5. Slice the fruit into tiny pieces.

6. Pour some oil into a basin.

7. Add some fruit and rice on top. Push lightly.

8. Spread red bean paste over it using a spoon.

9. Add another layer of rice and cherries.

10. Steam the bowl for 30 minutes in simmering water.

11. Combine the potato starch and water in a small bowl.

12. Mix thoroughly by stirring.

13. Combine the ingredients for the syrup and bring it to a boil. Boil for 10 minutes after adding starch water.

14. Lift the bowl from the water and place it inside the dish. On top, drizzle sweet syrup.

4.20 Chinese Almond Float Dessert

Cooking Time: 60 minutes

Serving Size: 6

Ingredients:

- 1 cup of cold water
- 1 can fruit cocktail with syrup
- 1 envelope unflavoured gelatine
- 2 teaspoons almond extract
- 1 cup evaporated milk
- 4 tablespoons granulated sugar
- 1 cup boiling water

Method:

1. Combine gelatine and sugar in a small bowl. Mix thoroughly.

2. Stir the gelatine mixture while adding the boiling water until the gelatine is completely dissolved.

3. Include milk, cold water, and almond essence. Mix thoroughly.

4. Permit the area to cool. Slice up and serve with canned fruit.

Chapter 5: Most Famous Chinese Dishes

5.1 Spicy Oyster Sauce Squid with Green Peppers

Cooking Time: 15 minutes

Serving Size: 2

Ingredients:

- 1 tablespoon low-sodium light soy
- sauce
- 1 green pepper (sliced into cubes)
- ½ teaspoon dark soy sauce
- 1 teaspoon oyster sauce
- 1 tablespoon rapeseed oil
- 1 medium white onion (cut into
- slices)
- 1 tablespoon fresh lemon juice
- A pinch of caster sugar
- 1 red chili (finely chopped)
- 200g whole baby squid (sliced into
- rings)
- 1 tablespoon rice vinegar

Method:

1. Add one tablespoon of oil to a hot wok.

2. Include onion slices and rapeseed oil. Heat till crisp and golden brown after 20 minutes.

3. Include red chilli and squid. Ten seconds of heating. Include rice vinegar.

4. Stir for a minute after adding the green pepper.

5. Add one tablespoon of water to the wok's edges to create steam.

6. Add the other ingredients and cook for an additional minute.

7. Stir, then serve right away.

5.2 Pineapple Chicken

Cooking Time: 12 minutes

Serving Size: 2

Ingredients:

- A pinch of black pepper
- 1 tablespoon cornflour
- ½ small pineapple (cubes)
- fresh coriander leaves (to garnish)
- 1 tablespoon rapeseed oil
- ½ red pepper (cubes)

- 250g boneless chicken thighs (sliced into cubes)
- sea salt flakes
- 1 spring onion (sliced)
- 2 dried chilies
- roasted cashew nuts

For the Sauce

- 1 teaspoon honey
- ¼ teaspoon Sriracha chili sauce
- 1 tablespoon cornflour
- 100ml pineapple juice
- 1 tablespoon light soy sauce
- 1 lime juice

Method:

1. Place the chicken in a big basin—salt & pepper to taste.

Corn flour should be added and combined. Place aside.

2. In a blender, combine all of the sauce's ingredients. Set aside.

3. Add the rapeseed oil to a wok that has been heated on high.

4. Stir in red chilli to provide flavour.

5. Stir in the chicken pieces for 5 minutes.

6. Include pineapple and red pepper. For 30 seconds, cook.

7. Stir in sauce and heat through stickiness.

8. Add the final ingredients and simmer for an additional 2 minutes.

9. Take the dish off the heat and top it with coriander leaves.

5.3 Buddha's Stir-Fried Mixed Vegetables

Cooking Time: 15 minutes

Serving Size: 2

Ingredients:

- 1 tablespoon rapeseed oil
- Ginger root (peeled and grated)
- 4 fresh shiitake mushrooms (dried
- and sliced)
- 1 cup dried wood ear mushrooms
- 1 cup of fresh beansprouts
- 1 medium carrot
- 1 cup of baby sweetcorn

- ½ teaspoon salted black beans
- (crushed with rice vinegar 1
- tablespoon)
- 1 can of bamboo shoots
- 2 spring onions (garnish)

For the Sauce

- 1 tablespoon light soy sauce
- 1 tablespoon vegetarian mushroom
- sauce
- 100 ml cold vegetable stock
- 1 teaspoon toasted sesame oil
- 1 tablespoon cornflour

Method:

1. Place all sauce ingredients in a blender and process until completely smooth.

Place aside.

2. Add the rapeseed oil to a wok that has been heated on high.

3. Add the ginger and cook on low. Cook the pasta and beans for one minute.

4. Add the remaining ingredients—all but the beansprout—to the vegetables. Stir thoroughly.

5. Add the sauce and stir until sticky, about 5 minutes.

6. Include the beansprout and cook for 30 seconds.

7. Move to a dish and add onion as a garnish.

5.4 Sichuan Hot Pot

Cooking Time: 1 hour 10 minutes
Serving Size: 1 hot pot

Ingredients:

For Soup Base

- 12-14 cups chicken stock
- 10 cloves garlic
- 1 cinnamon stick
- 2 tablespoons oil
- 10 cloves
- 1 tablespoon Sichuan peppercorns
- 10 whole red chilies
- 6 slices ginger
- 3-4 bay leaves
- 1 package spicy hot pot soup base
- 5-star anise

For Dipping Sauce

- Sesame seeds
- Peanuts
- Sesame paste
- Sesame oil
- Cilantro
- Soy sauce
- Chinese black vinegar
- Scallions
- Sacha sauce
- Chili oil
- Garlic

Hot Pot Sides

- Thinly shaved beef
- Sliced chicken
- Prepared frozen dumplings
- Chinese rice cakes
- Fresh noodles
- Assorted fish balls
- Thinly sliced fish fillets
- Napa cabbage
- Shiitake mushrooms
- Tofu sheets

- Glass noodles
- Firm tofu
- Soy puffs
- Straw mushrooms
- Green leaf lettuce
- Wood ear mushrooms

Method:

1. Heat a wok, then add the ginger and one tablespoon of oil.

2. Two minutes of stirring. Add the cloves, star anise, cinnamon stick, bay leaves, and garlic.

3. To develop flavours, cook for 5 minutes.

4. Include peppercorns, chiles, and a hot pot soup base. Cook for an additional 2 minutes.

5. After adding the chicken stock, wait until it boils. Transform into a big, deep pot. Place aside

6. Combine the dipping sauce's components and process until smooth. Set aside.

7. Get a hot plate and a plug ready. To boil, add the broth.

8. Add hot pot side components you enjoy and boil them for a few minutes.

9. Set the soup and dipping sauce. In the pot, serve.

5.5 Radish in Black Rice Vinegar with Crabmeat and Black Sesame Seeds

Cooking Time: 10 minutes

Serving Size: 2

Ingredients:

- 1 teaspoon rapeseed oil
- 5g black sesame seed (garnish)
- Dried chili flakes (garnish)
- 200g radishes (cut into slices)
- 1 tablespoon black rice vinegar
- 300g radish leaves
- A pinch of caster sugar
- 200g fresh white crab meat

Method:

1. Rapeseed oil is added to a hot wok that has been preheated. Allow 30 seconds to pass.

2. Add radish leaves and sliced radish to the wok.

3. Stir water around the wok's edges to create steam.

4. After 10 seconds of cooking, stir in the other ingredients.

5. Take the dish off the fire and serve it in another dish.

6. Sprinkle sesame seeds and chilli flakes on top of the radish.

5.6 Yang Chow Fried Rice

Cooking Time: 35 minutes
Serving Size: 6

Ingredients:

- 2 teaspoons salt
- 10 pieces shrimps
- 1 teaspoon garlic
- 3 tablespoons cooking oil
- ¼ cup green onion
- 2 pieces of raw eggs beaten
- 1 teaspoon sugar
- 6 cups cooked white rice
- 1 cup barbecued pork
- 1 ½ tablespoons soy sauce
- ¾ cup green peas
- 1 teaspoon ginger

Method:

1. Heat oil, ginger, and garlic in a pan.

2. Include the shrimp and boil them for 5 minutes. Place aside.

3. Stir the eggs for 30 seconds.

4. Completely combine the egg with the rice.

5. Include sugar, sauce, and other spices.

6. Add the meat from the BBQ and cook for 5 minutes.

7. Include green peas and shrimp. For five minutes, cook.

8. Add the green onions, then sauté them for one minute.

9. Place on a dish, then serve.

5.7 Wonton Soup

Cooking Time: 40 minutes

Serving Size: 6

Ingredients:

- 2 bok choy
- 2 cloves garlic
- 1 tablespoon ginger
- 4 cups chicken broth
- 3 green onions
- 1 tablespoon sesame oil
- 4 ounces shiitake mushrooms
- 1 tablespoon yellow miso paste

For Wontons

- 1 tablespoon reduced-sodium soy
- sauce
- 1 tablespoon ginger
- 1 tablespoon oyster sauce
- 1 teaspoon sesame oil
- 8 ounces medium shrimp
- 2 cloves garlic
- 2 green onions
- ½ teaspoon Sriracha
- ¼ teaspoon black pepper

- 36 wonton wrappers

Method:

1. Combine the garlic, ginger, shrimp, Sriracha, soy sauce, sesame oil, and oyster sauce in a bowl.

2. Place wonton wrappers on a plate and top with one tablespoon of the shrimp mixture.

3. Fold the wrappers and seal the edges.

4. Place a pan on a low flame and heat.

5. Include chicken broth, ginger, and garlic.

6. Add 2 cups of water, then boil.

7. Include the mushrooms and simmer for 10 minutes.

8. Add the miso paste, bok choy, and green onions. Cook for 3 minutes.

9. Stir for 2 minutes after adding the wonton.

10. Present warm with sauce.

5.8 Penang Curry with Chicken

Cooking Time: 35 minutes

Serving Size: 4

Ingredients:

- 2 peppers fresh red chili peppers
- ¼ cup fresh basil leaves
- 2 tablespoons palm sugar
- 4 cups of coconut milk
- ⅔ pound skinless (boneless and
- cubed)
- 2 tablespoons fish sauce
- 5 tablespoons Penang curry paste
- cooking oil
- 6 leaf kaffir lime leaves

Method:

1. Rapeseed oil is added to a hot wok that has been preheated.

2. Stir for 2 minutes after adding the curry paste.

3. Add the coconut milk and let it come to a boil.

4. Cook the chicken pieces for 15 minutes.

5. Stir for 2 minutes after adding the last few ingredients.

6. Add basil leaves as a garnish.

5.9 Peking Duck

Cooking Time: 1 hour 35 minutes
Serving Size: 4

Ingredients:

- ¼ teaspoon white pepper
- ⅛ teaspoon cloves
- ½ cup plum jam
- 3 tablespoons soy sauce
- 1 tablespoon honey
- 5 green onions
- 1 orange
- 1 tablespoon parsley
- 1 whole duck
- ½ teaspoon cinnamon
- ½ teaspoon ginger
- ¼ teaspoon nutmeg
- 1 ½ teaspoons sugar
- 1 ½ teaspoon white vinegar

Method:

1. Clean the inside and outside of the duck.

2. Combine cloves, ginger, nutmeg, white pepper, and cinnamon.

3. Season the duck with the spice mixture.

4. Pour one tablespoon of vinegar over the duck.

5. Spread with your hands, then chill for at least two hours.

6. Place water in a wok. For one hour, steam duck from the breast side.

7. Add green onions and lime juice.

8. Set the oven to 375 F.

9. After removing the duck's skin, place it in the pan to roast.

10. 30 minutes of roasting. Combine three tablespoons of soy sauce and honey.

11. Apply a light coating to the duck and cook for more than 10 minutes.

12. Combine the sugar, chutney, and vinegar to make the sauce.

13. Add orange slices and parsley as a garnish.

5. 10 Shrimp Rice Noodle Rolls

Cooking Time: 15 minutes
Serving Size: 8

Ingredients:

For Shrimp

- ½ teaspoon sugar
- ¼ teaspoon baking soda
- 2 tablespoons water
- ½ teaspoon cornstarch
- ¼ teaspoon sesame oil
- ¼ teaspoon salt
- 8 ounces shrimp
- ¼ teaspoon white pepper

For Sauce

- 1 teaspoon oyster sauce
- 1 teaspoon oil
- 2 teaspoons dark soy sauce
- 5 teaspoons sugar
- 1 scallion

- 6 slices ginger
- 2 ½ tablespoons light soy sauce
- ¼ cup of water
- Salt

For the Rice Noodle Rolls

- 1 cup of water
- Vegetable or canola oil
- 5 tablespoons rice flour
- 1 tablespoon mung bean starch
- 2 tablespoons wheat starch
- 2 tablespoons corn-starch
- ¼ teaspoon salt

Method:

1. Coat shrimp with water, sugar, and baking soda.

2. After two hours in the refrigerator, carefully wash.

3. Sprinkle shrimp with salt, white pepper, sesame oil, and cornstarch.

4. For an hour, cover and chill.

5. Combine all sauce ingredients and heat over a low flame.

6. Continue cooking until the mixture is smooth.

7. Soak a clean cloth in water, then set it aside.

8. After 10 minutes of steaming, place the shrimp in a bowl.

9. Include shrimp and rice noodles.

10. Roll up and cover with a damp cloth.

11. Take off the cloth and slice the rice noodles in half lengthwise.

12. Serve with sauce.

5.11 Chinese Buffet Green Beans

Cooking Time: 25 minutes

Serving Size: 6

Ingredients:

- 1-pound fresh green beans
- (trimmed)
- 2 tablespoons oyster sauce
- 2 teaspoons soy sauce
- 1 tablespoon oil sesame
- 2 cloves garlic (sliced)
- 1 tablespoon white sugar

Method:

1. Add sesame oil to a heated pan at a high temperature.

2. Include white sugar and garlic. Till brown, heat.

3. Include the other ingredients and green beans.

4. Bring to a boil, then simmer for 15 minutes to soften the beans.

5. Add sesame seeds as a garnish and serve.

5.12 Summer Special Shrimp and Fruit Fried Rice

Cooking Time: 60 minutes

Serving Size: 2

Ingredients:

- 6 halves walnuts
- 2 cups cold, cooked white rice
- 2 large eggs (beaten)
- 1 tablespoon vegetable oil
- 1 piece of ginger root
- 1 tablespoon soy sauce
- 2 tablespoons cilantro
- ⅔ cup fresh pineapple

- 2 red onions
- 3 green chili peppers
- ½ cup orange segments
- ½ pound shrimp
- salt and pepper

Method:

1. Add one tablespoon of oil to a heated wok and heat over medium heat.

2. Stir in the onion until it is golden. Place aside.

3. Add shrimp to a heated pan over high heat.

4. Stir continually for 10 minutes or until the mixture loses its pink hue. Set aside.

5. Clean the wok, then heat it on a high flame. Add one tablespoon of oil along with ginger, onion, and garlic.

6. Stir and cook for 3 minutes or until the edges are browned.

7. Include orange and pineapple. Stir the pineapple until it warms up.

8. Stir in the remaining ingredients. Add onion and shrimp. For three minutes, stir.

9. Add cilantro as a garnish and serve.

5.13 Vegetarian Hokkien Mee

Cooking Time: 22 minutes
Serving Size: 2

Ingredients:

- A knob of fresh ginger (grated)
- 100g Quorn mince
- 1 tablespoon low-sodium light soy
- sauce
- A drizzle of toasted sesame oil
- 1 tablespoon rapeseed oil
- 2 garlic cloves (chopped)
- 1 teaspoon dark soy sauce
- 2 mini sweet shallots (chopped)
- 1 red chili (chopped)
- 400g cooked egg noodles (200g
- dried)
- 100g fresh beansprouts
- 3 dried Chinese mushrooms
  (soaked and finely diced)
- 100ml hot vegetable stock

For Garnish

- Spring onions (sliced)
- Red chili (sliced into rings)

Method:

1. Heat the wok over high heat. Stir in the rapeseed oil.

2. Include shallots, garlic, ginger, and chile.

3. In the wok, heat and swirl to intensify flavours for one minute.

4. Include Quorn, mushrooms, and dark soy sauce. Take a two-minute break.

5. Include vegetable stock and soy sauce. For 10 minutes, cook.

6. Include the fried egg noodles and top them with sesame oil.

7. Mix well and serve.

8. You can serve the noodles in two bowls with the filling on top.

5.14 Beijing Egg and Tomato Noodle Soup

Cooking Time: 15 minutes

Serving Size: 2

Ingredients:

- 1 tablespoon vegetable bouillon powder
- 300g cooked rice noodles (150g uncooked)
- 250g tomatoes (cored and quartered)
- 100g Chinese cabbage (cut into slices)
- 1 tablespoon sesame oil
- 1 tablespoon light soy sauce
- A pinch of white pepper
- 1 egg (beaten)
- 2 spring onions (sliced, to garnish)
- 1 root ginger (peeled and grated)
- 5 fresh shiitake mushrooms (dried and cut into slices)

Method:

1. Add tomato paste, ginger, garlic, mushrooms, and veggie powder to a hot wok.

2. Fill the wok with 1 litre of water and bring it to a boil.

3. Cook the vegetables for 2 minutes or until they are tender.

4. Bring to a simmer and stir in rice noodles. Add sesame oil and soy sauce.

5. Stir in the remaining ingredients.

6. Stir continuously for 2 minutes after adding the beaten eggs.

7. Quickly take the pan off the heat and serve.

5.15 Braised Pork Ball in Gravy

Cooking Time: 15 minutes

Serving Size: 4

Ingredients:

For Meatballs

- 1 teaspoon salt
- 1 tablespoon dark soy sauce
- 100-gram corn starch
- 1000-gram pork
- 1 leftover steamed bun
- scallion 20 grams
- 2 tablespoon light soy sauce
- 2 tablespoon Shaoxing wine

- 1 cup oil
- 2-gram ginger

For Sauce

- Sugar ¼ tablespoon
- Corn starch 1 tablespoon
- Dark soy sauce ¼ tablespoon
- 2 slices fresh ginger
- Light soy sauce ½ tablespoon
- Water 1 cup

Method:

1. Add the ingredients for the meatballs to a pan and stir them steadily in one direction for five minutes.

2. Form little meatballs that are elongated and circular.

3. Combine all of the sauce's components in a wok or skillet.

4. Stir for 10 minutes while adding oil.

5. After adding, fry the meatballs for 30 seconds.

Serve hot alongside rice.

5.16 Steamed Garlic Prawns with Vermicelli

Cooking Time: 17 minutes

Serving Size: 2

Ingredients:

- 10 tiger prawns
- 2 tablespoon light soy sauce
- ¼ teaspoon sugar
- 1 tablespoon cooking oil
- 100 g mung bean vermicelli noodles
- 1 tablespoon water
- 2 tablespoon minced garlic
- 2 tablespoon chopped fresh chili
- 1 tablespoon Shaoxing rice wine
- ¼ teaspoon white pepper
- 1 pinch salt
- scallions for garnishing

Method:

1. Soak the noodles and add one tablespoon of oil to prevent sticking. Set aside.

2. Peel and cut the prawns. Serve them with noodles.

3. Add oil to the hot pan. Rice wine, soy sauce, sugar, chile, white pepper, and garlic should all be added. Five minutes of heating is required to flavour.

4. Pour sauce over the noodles and prawns.

5. After 5 minutes of steaming, serve hot.

5.17 Mapo Tofu

Cooking Time: 35 minutes

Serving Size: 6

Ingredients:

- ¼ teaspoon sugar
- 6-8 dried red chilies
- 1 ½ tablespoon Sichuan peppercorns
- 3 tablespoons ginger
- 3 tablespoons garlic
- ¼ cup low sodium chicken broth
- 1-pound silken tofu
- 1 scallion
- ½ cup oil
- 1-2 fresh chili peppers
- 1 ½ teaspoons corn-starch
- ¼ teaspoon sesame oil
- 8 ounces pork

- 1-2 tablespoons spicy bean sauce

Method:

1. Add chillies to oil in a hot wok. For the fragment, stir for five minutes. Place aside.

2. Add oil to a heated wok. Add the ginger, garlic, and peppercorns. For 7 minutes, cook.

3. Include ground pork and boil it until the pink colour has vanished.

4. Include the chicken broth and bean mixture. Stir thoroughly.

5. Combine corn-starch and water. Add to the bean mixture after mixing.

6. Include the final components and seasonings. For ten minutes, stir.

7. Serve hot with onion as a garnish.

5.18 Lobster Tails, Baby Asparagus, and Eggs in Hot Bean Sauce

Cooking Time: 15 minutes

Serving Size: 2

Ingredients:

- 1 teaspoon cornflour
- 2 spring onions
- 100ml hot vegetable stock
- 1 egg (beaten)
- 1 tablespoon rapeseed oil
- 2 garlic cloves (chopped)
- 200g cooked fresh lobster (sliced into cubes)
- 100g baby asparagus spears
- 1 teaspoon yellow bean paste
- ½ teaspoon dark soy sauce
- 1 tablespoon light soy sauce
- 1 ginger (peeled and grated)
- 1 red chili (chopped)

Method:

1. Rapeseed oil is added to a hot wok that has been preheated. For five minutes, toss.

2. Add the ginger, garlic, and chile to release flavour. Stir for 2 minutes.

3. Stir for a minute after adding the lobsters. For an additional minute, stir in the asparagus.

4. Add one tablespoon of water to the wok's edges to create steam.

5. Include the two types of soy sauce. Add yellow bean paste after stirring.

6. Stir in the egg and bring it to a boil.

7. Add the cornflour to the wok after combining it with two tablespoons of water.

8. Keep stirring until the mixture thickens.

9. Add onions as a garnish and serve right away.

Conclusion

Chinese cuisine is highly well-known and offers all the nutrients needed by the body and metabolism to stay healthy. Chinese people do not have an obesity problem despite consuming an average of 30% more calories than Americans and following the same behavioural patterns. This is so because Chinese eating avoids foods high in sugar and low in vitamins. Chinese cuisine is primarily prepared via frying, deep-frying, steaming, boiling, and roasting.

Chinese food prepared at home differs significantly from that served in restaurants. Chinese food has a lot of health advantages. Your bodily fluids are better controlled, and your metabolism is improved. Chinese cuisine is well-known in America for its flavours and cooking techniques. Due to the vast range of cooking methods used, vegetarians, lacto-Ovo-vegetarians, Buddhists, and Ovo-vegetarians can consume Chinese food. Try out these various Chinese recipes to enjoy Chinese food on your table.